Amazing Biomes

GRASSLANDS

BROWN BEAR BOOKS

Published by Brown Bear Books Ltd

4877 N. Circulo Bujia
Tucson, AZ 85718
USA

and

First Floor
9-17 St. Albans Place
London N1 0NX

© 2015 Brown Bear Books Ltd

ISBN: 978-1-78121-242-4

Library of Congress Cataloging-in-Publication Data
available upon request

Author: Leon Gray
Designer: Karen Perry
Picture Researcher: Clare Newman
Editor: Tim Harris
Children's Publisher: Anne O'Daly
Design Manager: Keith Davis
Editorial Director: Lindsey Lowe

Manufactured in the United States of America

CPSIA compliance information: Batch# AG/5567

Picture Credits

The photographs in this book are used by permission
and through the courtesy of:

T=Top, C=Center, B=Bottom, L=Left, R=Right

Front cover: FLPA/Bernd Rohrschneider.
Interior: 1, ©Pavel Svoboda/Shutterstock;
4-5, ©Michal Bednarek/Shutterstock; 5tr, ©Johan
Swanepoel/Shutterstock; 6tl, ©Pictureguy/
Shutterstock; 6bl, ©Vadim Petrakov/Shutterstock;
6br, ©Grobler du Preez/Shutterstock; 6tr, ©Tyrin/
Shutterstock; 6br, ©Utosr/Shutterstock; 8-9, ©Michal
Bednarek/Shutterstock; 9c, ©Erichon/Shutterstock;
10-11, ©Miverva Studio/Shutterstock;
11tr, ©Elistudio/Shutterstock; 12-13, ©Graeme
Shannon/Shutterstock; 13cl, ©Jukgrapong/
Shutterstock; 13cr, ©Inaki Caperochipi/Age Fotostock/
Alamy; 14, ©Domonique de la Croix/Shutterstock;
15tl, ©Nazzu/Shutterstock; 15tr, ©David Thyberg/
Shutterstock; 15b, ©Timothy Epp/Shutterstock;
16bl, ©eClick/Shutterstock; 16cr, ©Tarabird/
Shutterstock; 17, ©Villiers Steyn/shutterstock;
18bl, ©Gualtiero Boffi/Shutterstock; 18/19,
©Moizhusen/Shutterstock; 19tc, ©Bridgena Barnard/
Shutterstock; 20cl, ©Christian Vinces/Shutterstock;
20-21, © Mark Ralston/AFP/Getty Images; 21t, ©Asiir/
Wikipedia; 22, ©Tom Koene/Horizons WWP/Alamy;
23t, ©B Brown/Shutterstock; 23b, ©Aleksandrhunta/
Shutterstock; 24c, ©Byelikova Oksana/Shutterstock;
24/25, ©Pavel Svoboda/Shutterstock; 25tr, ©Philip
Perry/FLPA; 26b, ©Corbis; 26-27, © Latitude/Corbis;
27t, ©Ypalmer 45/Dreamstime; 28cl, ©Utosr/
Shutterstock; 28cr, ©Nazzu/Shutterstock;
28bl, ©Aleksandrhunta/Shutterstock;
28-29, ©Michal Bednarek/Shutterstock;
29tl, ©Ypalmer 45/Dreamstime;
29bl, ©Bridgena Barnard/Shutterstock.

Brown Bear Books has made every attempt to contact
the copyright holder. If you have any information
please contact licensing@brownbearbooks.co.uk

All other photographs and artworks © Brown Bear Books Ltd.

Contents

• • • • • • • • • • • • • • • • →

INTRODUCTION

Some parts of the world are large, open areas of land covered in grass. These places are called grasslands. They sometimes have a few trees scattered across them.

The places where animals or plants live and grow are called **biomes**. Some animals and plants live in deserts, tropical forests, or oceans. And some have **adapted** to survive in grasslands.

Not all grasslands are the same. Some are in hot, **tropical** parts of the world. There are tropical grasslands in Africa, South America, and Australia. **Temperate** grasslands are different. They get cold in winter and are found in North America, Central Asia, and Argentina.

Read on to find out what grasslands are like—and how plants, animals, and people live in them.

Lions live in tropical grasslands in Africa. This male is sitting in long grass.

EAST AFRICA

This tropical grassland is in Tanzania, in East Africa. Some acacia trees grow among the grass. The mountain in the distance is named Kilimanjaro.

GRASSLANDS OF

The grasslands of the world are called different names: **prairies** in North America, **steppes** in Central Asia, and **savannas** in Africa.

Many prairies in North America have been made into farmland.

NORTH AMERICA

Capybaras live on the Llanos grasslands in Venezuela.

SOUTH AMERICA

Gemsbok oryx live on the savanna in southern Africa. Sadly, they are often hunted for their horns.

THE WORLD

Temperate grassland

Tropical grassland

ASIA

EUROPE

The people of the steppes in Kazakhstan were some of the first people to tame and ride wild horses.

AFRICA

AUSTRALIA

These strange rocks are called the Bungle Bungles. They rise high above the Purnululu grasslands in Australia.

ANTARCTICA

CLIMATE

Grasslands form in areas where there is not enough rain during the whole year for forests to grow. Tropical grasslands have more rain than deserts, even though they are nearly as hot. Temperate grasslands can be baking hot in summer, but they are also freezing cold in winter.

GREEN GRASS

Serengeti National Park in East Africa is a tropical grassland. It is very green in the wet season. At this time, the animals eat grass and drink from small pools.

Tropical grasslands occur in places where there is heavy rainfall for half the year (the wet season) and very little or no rain at all for the other half of the year (the dry season). During the wet season, the grass grows tall and green.

In the dry season, life becomes harder for zebras and other animals that eat grass. They must travel to places where the grass is greener.

During the dry season, the rain stops and the grasslands suffer **drought**. The sun beats down. Daytime temperatures often reach 104°F (40°C). The grass turns as dry as dust. **Grazing** animals have to travel to search for food. After about six months, the rains come again.

Extreme Weather

The steppes of Central Asia and the prairies of North America are temperate grasslands. The prairies in Oklahoma also often reach temperatures of more than 104°F (40°C) in August.

Ferocious winds called **tornadoes** sometimes speed across the prairies. The wind in a tornado may blow at 300 miles per hour (480 kilometers per hour). A tornado's wind is strong enough to destroy everything in its path. In winter, tornadoes can whip snowstorms into blizzards that form deep drifts.

TORNADOES

Every year, hundreds of tornadoes tear across the prairies of the United States. Tornadoes often form when cold air and warm air meet.

WOW!

● Ulaanbaatar is on the Central Asian steppes. In spring, the temperature at dawn is a below freezing 23°F (−5°C) but rises to 86°F (30°C) in the afternoon.

● Winnipeg, in the Canadian prairies, has recorded a temperature of −54°F (−47.8°C), almost as cold as Antarctica.

A shepherd looks after his sheep on a snowy steppe in Central Asia during the winter.

Coping with Cold

Temperate grassland animals have adapted to survive the icy winter weather. Bison have shaggy, windproof fur that grows very thick in the winter. Groups of bison huddle together for warmth on the coldest days. Some smaller mammals, snakes, tortoises, and lizards dig burrows in the ground. There, they go into a state of deep sleep called **hibernation**.

PLANTS

Grassland plants have to be tough. In tropical grasslands, plants are scorched by the sun and eaten by zebras and antelope. In temperate grasslands, they are buried by snow in winter. But grasses are survivors and grow back.

BROWSERS

Some trees that grow on tropical African savannas have an unusual shape. They never have leaves close to the ground. This is because leaves low down would be eaten by elephants, giraffes, and other **browsers**.

At the end of the wet season, tropical grassland is lush and green. Flowers also appear, covering the ground in a carpet of blue, purple, red, and yellow. When the dry season comes a few months later, the flowers die, and the grass turns the color of straw.

In the wet season, flame lilies bloom in East Africa's tropical savanna.

Stem

Elephant's Foot Plant

This plant grows on grasslands in Madagascar, an island off the east coast of Africa. Its fat stem looks a little bit like the foot of an elephant. The stem can store a lot of water to help the plant survive through the dry season.

Amazing Grass

Whether in tropical or temperate grassland, grass is an amazing survivor. On North American prairies, the tallest grasses grow to 6.5 feet (2 meters) high. Grasses on the African savanna grow even taller. In the wet season, they quickly shoot up to 10 feet (3 meters). In the dry season, the only part of the grass that stays alive is the root.

Unlike most plants, grasses grow well if they are grazed by animals—as long as the animals don't eat the roots.

BIO FACT

Shrubs and trees such as acacias and baobabs grow in tropical grasslands. Not many trees or shrubs grow in temperate grasslands.

In spring, a carpet of colorful flowers covers a grassland in South Africa.

Thin trunk in dry season

Fat trunk in wet season

Baobab trees soak up large amounts of water in the wet season. They store the water in their trunks. Their trunks are fat in the wet season and thinner in the dry season.

Indian Paintbrush

The Indian paintbrush is a plant that lives on the prairies of North America. The red parts of the plant are leaves, not flowers. The tiny flowers are hidden among the leaves. The Indian paintbrush can grow in dry soil. It is also a plant that fights for its life. Its roots grab the roots of the plant next to it and steal the water. A plant that does this is called a parasite.

ANIMALS

Tropical grassland **herbivores**, such as zebras, wildebeest, and impalas, love to graze on juicy green grass. As the herbivores feed, cheetahs, lions, and other **predators** watch them.

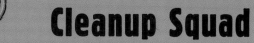

Cleanup Squad

Vultures feed on the **carcasses** of animals that have died. They stick their long necks deep inside the bodies of dead animals to rip off pieces of flesh. When a lion or hyena has finished eating its "kill," vultures swiftly move in to pick at the bones.

Impalas are always on their guard when they drink from waterholes. If they see a lion or crocodile, they are ready to spring away quickly—but some might be unlucky!

Millions of herbivores feed on grasslands. There is usually plenty to eat, and grass is packed with nutrients, so herbivores do well. Their bodies can **digest** grass—but other animals are not so lucky. They cannot digest grass or other plants, so they have to eat meat to survive. When the dry season comes and the herbivores move on, their predators must follow them.

ELEPHANTS

Elephants live in the tropical grasslands of Africa. They eat grass and leaves, and they drink when they find water. Adult elephants are too large for most predators to attack them.

Tropical Predators

Large herds of grazing animals live in constant danger from predators, but there is some safety in numbers—with more eyes and ears on the lookout for danger. Predators that hunt in groups, such as lions, hyenas, and wolves, are easier to spot, but cheetahs usually hunt alone. Spotted hyenas hunt young wildebeest, antelope, and zebras. They need 7 pounds (3 kilograms) of meat a day. Lions eat animals as big as young rhinos. A male lion needs to eat 15 pounds (7 kilograms) of meat a day.

A spotted hyena watches over the East African savanna. This predator kills zebras, wildebeest, and smaller animals.

Zebras often graze with wildebeest.

The wildebeest is the most common large animal on the African savanna.

Superfast Hunters

Cheetahs are the fastest animals in the world. They can sprint at 60 miles per hour (100 km/h). The quickest person can run at 23 miles per hour (37 km/h). Cheetahs mainly hunt gazelles, young wildebeest, and smaller prey. A cheetah can only sprint at top speed for about 30 seconds. If it can't catch its prey in that time, it may go hungry!

MIGRATION

More than one million wildebeest **migrate** from the Serengeti grassland, in Tanzania, when the dry season begins. They move to the Maasai Mara, in Kenya, where there is more water and the grass is greener. Zebras also travel with them.

19

Burrowing owls live in temperate grasslands in North America. Because there are few trees to nest in, they make their homes in burrows.

Temperate Grazers

Pronghorn antelopes graze on the grasslands of North America. They can run extremely fast if they need to escape hunting coyotes. At one time, millions of bison also roamed the American prairies. Most American plains bison were shot by people for meat and skins in the nineteenth and twentieth centuries, although a few thousand survive today. Deer, goats, and wild Przewalski's horses eat the grass on the steppes of Central Asia. The horses are endangered because there is now less land for them to roam on.

Prairie Dogs

On the treeless prairies of North America, the only place prairie dogs can live is in burrows in the ground. Many prairie dogs live in each "town" of underground tunnels. There, they are safe from hunting hawks and eagles, and can survive the bitter winter. Lots of other animals live in the prairie dogs' burrows, too, including rabbits and snakes.

Przewalski's horse is the only kind of truly wild horse. It has never been tamed for riding. About 400 of these animals live on the steppes of China and Mongolia.

BIO FACT

At one time, a prairie dog "town" on grassland in Texas was thought to house 400 million animals. There is now less grassland, and so there are fewer prairie dogs.

PEOPLE

Can you imagine living out on the grasslands? You may find yourself many miles from the nearest town. If you had animals, you would always be on the move in search of green grass for them. And if you lived on the steppes or prairies, you would have to deal with bitterly cold weather in the winter.

THE MAASAI

The Maasai are **seminomadic** people who live and tend to their animals on the grasslands of Kenya, East Africa.

Native North American people have lived on the temperate grasslands of North America for many centuries. Some of these people once survived by hunting bison for food and clothing. Most of the prairies where bison once roamed have now been turned into farmland. Farmers plow the land to grow crops. The grassland is also used as **pasture** for cattle.

- Farming has gradually taken over much of what used to be grassland.

Steppe People

The easiest way for people to travel across the vast steppes of Central Asia is on horseback. There are not many roads or railroads, and horses are good at walking over rough ground.

Grass Fires

At the end of the dry season, the grass is very dry, and bush fires start easily. However, farmers also often set fire to the grass on purpose. They know that fresh green grass will grow back quickly. Fresh grass makes better food for their animals.

Tourism

Tourism is popular in some tropical grasslands. Every year, millions of people visit Africa's national parks to see the lions and other animals. Park rangers look after the animals and protect them from **poachers**.

The biggest tourist attractions on temperate grasslands are in North America, where people visit Native American settlements, festivals, and bison **reserves**.

A park ranger in Kenya with an **orphaned** black rhinoceros. The rhino has just been released back into the wild.

YURT CAMP
Horses graze on grasslands at a camp on the Central Asian steppes. Circular tents like these are called yurts.

THE FUTURE

Earth's climate is changing. Some grasslands are drying out due to lack of rain. They may become deserts. At the same time, some deserts are getting more rain and may turn into grasslands.

As the number of people in the world gets bigger, more grasslands are planted with crops to feed them. **Overgrazing** by farm animals and the growth of towns crowd out the wild animals.

Not all the news about grasslands is bad, though. Many new nature reserves have been created. New towns can't be built in them, and their grasslands can't be plowed. The plants and animals still have some places to live.

The increasing size of cities, such as Cape Town in South Africa, means there is less space for animals.

This grassland has suffered a drought. If the drought lasts a long time, the land may become a desert.

LIONS

Here is a female lion, or lioness, and her cub. Lions need tropical grasslands in Africa, so that they can hunt and raise their families. If the grasslands go, then so will the lions.

QUIZ

Look at these pictures and see if you can answer the questions. The answers are on page 31.

1 What is the name of these strange-looking rocks in Australia?

2 These trees grow on African grasslands. Can you name them?

3 On which grasslands have people bred horses for hundreds of years?

4 What might a grassland turn into if it doesn't get any rain?

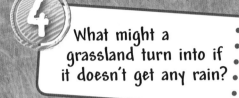

Fact File

- Africa has more tropical grassland than any other continent. It covers half of Africa's land surface.

- Brazil's tropical grassland is called cerrado. The state of Wyoming could fit into the cerrado almost ten times!

- A huge area of temperate grassland, or steppe, stretches from Ukraine to northern China—a third of the way around the world.

5 This animal can run faster than any other. What is it?

Winners and Losers

⬆ In some places, African elephant numbers are now on the increase because more people are protecting them in these areas.

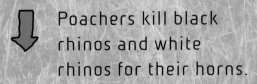

⬇ Poachers kill black rhinos and white rhinos for their horns.

GLOSSARY

adapted: When a plant or animal has changed to help it cope better in its surroundings.

biomes: The places where plants or animals usually live and grow.

browsers: Animals that eat the leaves and fruits of trees and shrubs.

carcasses: The bodies of dead animals.

digest: When an animal's body breaks down food to make energy.

drought: When it doesn't rain at all for a long time.

graze: To bite off and eat grass. Deer, impalas, wildebeest, and zebras all graze. They are called grazers.

herbivores: Animals that eat grass and other plants.

hibernation: The time when animals go into a very deep sleep. This usually happens in the winter.

migrate: To travel from one place to another in search of food.

orphaned: An animal whose parents have died or been killed.

overgrazing: Occurs when there are too many animals in an area, so grass cannot grow again after being grazed.

pasture: Grass for feeding animals such as cattle, horses, and sheep.

poachers: People who kill wild animals when it is against the law.

prairies: Huge grassy plains in central Canada and the United States.

predators: Animals that catch and eat other animals.

prey: Animals that are hunted by other animals called predators.

reserves: Land put aside for plants and wild animals to live in.

savanna: Tropical grasslands with few trees found in tropical Africa.

seminomadic: Relating to people who travel seasonally and grow crops.

steppes: Huge grassy plains in Asia and eastern Europe.

temperate: Areas of Earth between the hot tropics and cold polar regions.

tornadoes: Very strong winds that sweep across the countryside under thunderclouds.

tropical: The areas of Earth on either side of the equator. Tropical places are very warm or hot all year.

FURTHER RESOURCES

Books

Callery, Shaun. *Life Cycles: Grassland.* New York: Kingfisher, 2011.

Carney, Elizabeth. *Big Cats: Pictures to Purr About and Info to Make You Roar!* (National Geographic Kids Everything). Washington, DC: National Geographic Children, 2011.

Gibson, Karen Bush. *Native American History for Kids: With 21 Activities.* Chicago: Chicago Review Press, 2010.

Patkau, Karen. *Who Needs a Prairie?: A Grassland Ecosystem* (Ecosystem Series). Plattsburg, NY: Tundra Books, 2014.

Web Sites

Pittsburgh Zoo: African Savanna
www.pittsburghzoo.org/animallist.aspx?c=2
Check out the African savanna pages of the Pittsburgh Zoo, which offer in-depth information on the life cycles of the springbok, African lion, black rhinoceros, sacred ibis, the rare Amur leopard, and more.

Prairie Wildlife Research
www.prairiewildlife.org/whatwedo
Find out all about endangered species recovery across North America's vast, natural grasslands. With fascinating videos, photos, and text.

Serengeti National Park
www.serengeti.org
Visit the dramatic landscapes and experience the sights and sounds of wild animals on the site of the world's most famous tropical grasslands.

World Wildlife Fund: Great Plains
www.worldwildlife.org/places/northern-great-plains
Take a look at the Native American peoples and indigenous animals of the Northern Great Plains of Canada and the United States. Discover what is being done to help conserve these spectacular biomes.

Answers to the Quiz: **1** The Bungle Bungles. **2** Baobab trees. **3** The steppes of Kazakhstan. **4** A desert. **5** A cheetah.

INDEX